EX-CETERA
HLR

Published by Nine Pens Press
2023
www.ninepens.co.uk

ISBN: 978-1-7391517-5-1
019

For my girls

x

Dolly

At the start I was your precious little paper doll.
You would dress me up & parade me around,

fix me up smart, paint bright lipsticked grins on me
to fit your vision of vivacity. I felt special hanging

off your arm, dazzling at soirées, our evenings frittered away
eating microscopic canapés & chatting to people far richer,

saner, better than me. Then you unfolded me & discovered
the concertinaed versions of me—the layers of conflict

-ing personalities, all of the wildly oscillating
moods that consumed me, the cinematic series

of traumatic events that had condemned me to a life
of cyclical misery—&, where all my various fucked-up

paper selves hold hands, there are the creases: raised scars
formed when I was living in the back pockets & wallets

of all those bad men who came before you. At first you tried
to laminate me in a glossy sheen, to coat me in hard varnish

to protect me, but my tattered paper body was already
disintegrating. When you met me, I was *so close* to falling

apart completely. It took nothing for me to be ripped to shreds.
& I believe my fragility was, secretly, part of what drew you to me;

I was primed to satisfy your saviour complex, to make a hero
out of you. Now, all these years later, my body is glazed

in sticky memories & I've been left with an echo of your voice
in my crumpled head — your voice, the soundtrack to my rise

& fall, summoning me across dancehalls & galleries, rousing
me from infinity-loop nightmares & asinine daydreams, promising

me that you'll love me forever, that you'll never leave me, waking
me in another hospital bed after another attempt, calling me *Dolly*.

First Things First

How did we get here?
Well, you saw a photograph of me
in a magazine & said, *I have to know her.*
We met by chance in a dark room some months later.
You said, *I'm so pleased that you look nothing like you
do in that picture* & thus the muddled parameters
of our unbounding love were set.

x

We left together & went to Vingt-Quatre on the Fulham Road. Over an
endless procession of drinks, we spoke for hours, about *Dead Man's
Shoes*; Sixto Rodriguez; the generation of older women who have poorly
drawn dolphin tattoos; Copenhagen in the summertime; the Kray
twins; the invention of the blackest black paint; where to get the best
fish & chips; the Silva Mind Control Method; pulling teeth (physically
& metaphorically); *The Glass Bead Game*; the Iraq war; pilates;
grasshoppers; how you can tell a lot about a person from the state of
their butter; the perfect way to die. You knew things about me that I'd
long forgotten. We left without paying the bill.

x

I only realised my nose was bleeding
when the champagne in my glass turned pink. You said
it suited me, told me I *should have nosebleeds more often.*

x

Whenever I'd done a runner from restaurants before, us offenders (fed-up teens sick of languishing in poverty, desperate to experience the novelty of eating A Nice Meal for once in our tragic lives) would always collapse in hysterics, breathless, hiding around a corner expecting to be nabbed by police. We'd feel like we'd gotten away with murder, be buzzing off our minor crime for hours after. But with you, we left so casually—no prior planning, no scheming, just walked out calmly—& neither of us acknowledged what we'd done: ripped off VQ Chelsea for some £700. This set a precedent. It was as if we both felt that the world owed us something. Like life was ours for the taking.

x

I never mentioned my boyfriend.
I didn't have to: I dumped him
the next day. *For* you. For *you*.

x

Every day that I didn't have a nosebleed I felt like I'd disappointed you, let you down, failed you somehow. But I bled for you in so many other ways, spent so much of my time willing my body to bend to impossible angles for you, served my soul up on a silver platter for you to devour.

This is what traumatised borderlines do: we give everything, *every thing*, to everyone, or else nothing at all—walls up, mute, collapsing inward on ourselves. But I bled for the love of it, for the love of us, of this, of you. I haemorrhaged emotionally—stood stockstill in the ruby pool of my ardency, my soles tacky with immovable devotion, ready to traipse a trail of claret footprints all over the city so that you could always find me—knowing that I'd bleed out fully in the end, but believing it worth it: for the moment, for the poetry, for the memory, for the experience of having loved & been loved at all.

Frankly, exsanguination had never felt so good.

Brent Cross Shopping Centre

On our third date, we went shopping for funeral outfits.

We bought the charcoal pinstripe suit that you'll wear at yours
with a credit card we'd pilfered from my neighbour's mail.
You stole the dress that I'll wear at mine, harried it into a ball
and shoved it up your t-shirt, left the shop pregnant, glowing
with the success of impressing me, of making me happy.

That dress is the most beautiful, perfect possession I own.
Pale pink bodice, the colour of slight embarrassment; sweetheart
neckline to make my post-obit tits look great; intricate black lace
overlay and nipped-in waist; the buzz of our new love ingrained
in the fibres of its floor-length sheer skirts. "Now you'll be perfect
in life *and* in death," you said, your eyes flickering, feral.

Yes, I'd have been anything, whatever
you wanted me to be. Hidden in a suitcase
under my bed to keep it pristine, I sometimes take
the dress out just to look at it, to touch it, to make
sure it still exists. I am *so* excited to wear it.

That night, I wrote you a note on a Rizla cigarette paper,
my looping handwriting in purple ink, evidence of my essential
tremor betrayed in the curvature of the letters: *O*s quivering, capital
I lurching, seasick. I tucked it into the pocket of your suit jacket
when you were taking out the bins. Either you'll be buried
with it, or you'll find it when I'm dead. I know you
haven't discovered it yet because, if you had, things would be
so very different and I wouldn't have to write poems like this.

This Is Love Like

This is love like sucking lemon juice out of your papercuts & ignoring aeroplane safety demonstrations. Like ridiculous wine descriptions & waking up on Turnpike Lane with two black eyes, dress drenched in dew. Like four-day stubble & *you're bang in trouble, young lady*. Like every rhetorical question that's ever been answered in earnest & dancing on infinite eggshells. Like freshly ironed Hugo Boss shirts & seamless morphine dreams. Like scrunched-up betting slips & *You have 196 missed calls*. Like swimming from London to Mexico & believing in angels. Like the sound of chattering teeth & huffing glue in a car park. Like *don't fucking touch me*. Like disappearing acts & swapping house keys. Like antiseptic applied too late & the type of anticipation that makes you vomit. Like fortnightly overdoses & falling asleep in the bath, then coming round choking on grey water, soap bubbles up your nose. Like a bookcase with no shelves & pinching each other because we can't believe we're actually alive. Like a cloud of watermelon vape smoke & eating sugared doughnuts with a knife & fork. Like rusty kisses & missing the last bus home. Like *never let me go.* Like taking LSD & meeting the ghost of Keats on Hampstead Heath. Like primal scream therapy & duty-free toffee vodka. Like cheap tinned peaches & the engineering feat of bascule bridges. Like coffin shopping & an error in a cryptic crossword clue. Like a stolen bottle of mustard in a handbag & every Irish funeral. Like drinking a bottle of Coke & immediately eating a Mento. Like the relief when the pregnancy test is negative & the horror when it means I've just gotten fat. Like *we're bad for each other.* Like feeling more inspired standing outside the house my favourite writer killed herself in than the house in which she lived. Like a marriage proposal in the frozen aisle at Tesco & losing the back of an earring. Like relying too heavily on answers garnered from an upturned glass shifting gracelessly across a Ouija board. Like speaking Nadsat unironically. Like *you're the best thing that's ever happened to me.*

Like overflowing ashtrays & buying sunflowers just to watch them die. Like a scratched *Blonde on Blonde* vinyl snagging on the needle & an itemised list of every bruise I've ever had. Like shark fin soup for the psychotic soul & forever picking mystery greens out of your teeth. Like crushing white beetles under black Nike Blazers & arranging their powdered exoskeletons into heart-shaped piles. Like throwing Carol Ann Duffy's *New Selected Poems* at me in the street & snapping the head off a Cornish pixie. Like relaxing on concrete beaches & getting an erection in a cemetery. Like *l'appel du vide,* constantly. Like crunching your way through the fat stack of candy necklaces throttling my larynx & spitting the pieces into my bellybutton because you're suddenly diabetic. Like having your fuckfest interrupted by a Jehovah's Witness wanting to give you a pamphlet that tells you you're fucked in a non fun way, *unless.* Like an overwhelming desire to go to the aquarium & 'halloumi' autocorrecting to 'hallucinations'. Like tattooing your knuckles with the tip of my tongue & waking up totally exhausted after twelve hours of uninterrupted sleep. Like falling & forgetting & failing & faking & flailing & *Fuck Forever*-ing. Like torture, like nirvana, this is love like a death. A glorious death. The most magnificent. The absolute worst. Excruciating.

Gagged & Bound

Sometimes I didn't talk at all.
That depression served like a gagging order,
thick cotton wool packed down my gullet,
my smile flatlined, rubbing silence like
sandpaper against the smooth roof
of my mouth, a tube of superglue applied as lipstick,
things I want to say deep down in my stomach
but pointless, it's all pointless, or worse
sometimes no words left, no words at all,
no language for this sadness, just blankness
& crying with no noise & staring at walls
for days at a time & can't look you in the eye
& *want* to die & want to *die*.

Most times I'd tell you interesting facts
about ketchup & painters & space,
Japan & coins & pregnant giraffes,
but sometimes I didn't talk at all,
sometimes for a long time,
days or weeks unable to speak,
unable to prise my lips apart
to answer when you call me Dolly,
to reply when you ask me, *Are you okay?*

But still you'd wait & wait,   still,
with the patience of a saint,
until I came back,

until I came back to tell you that
There's a treasure chest containing $1million
buried somewhere in the Rocky Mountains
& then I'd get excited because I'd decided
that we absolutely *had* to find it
& then I'd cry because you'd remind me that
With our records, babe,
America would never let us in
& then the silence would begin
again. But still you'd wait & wait,   still,
with the patience of a saint
until I came back to you.

Worried to Death (1)

There was an inexplicable period when
we'd always drink a bottle of champagne before bed,

sometimes two. A ludicrous luxury; unsustainable,
silly. I did not recognise myself but joined in gladly.

There was something different about fucking tipsy
on Perrier-Jouët—something glistening, elevated, fizzy.

I don't know where you found the money to support all those
popped corks. I never asked. Better to ignore my ignorance.

We'd always drink a bottle of champagne before bed.
We worried about those who didn't: those who didn't drink

a bottle of champagne before bed & those who didn't worry.
You believed we were living the dream—though whose, exactly,

I can't say. You'd say, *Look at us, young & beautiful*
& in love & having so much fun, but I worried

constantly, generalised anxiety & dread & panic
rotting the soft parts of me. You worried

about politics & justice & inequality & about me, justifiably.
Once I woke up to you checking my pulse, my breathing, fearing

I'd taken too many quetiapine tablets again & died in my sleep.
The risk was always there: suicidal tendencies, the shit-stirring

third wheel of this party. Maybe that's why you'd make us drink
champagne so frequently: to celebrate my body's tenacity,

how it always refused to die, how it stubbornly clung on to being
alive despite my litany of efforts to render myself otherwise.

We'd always drink a bottle of champagne before bed:
it reminded us that we weren't quite dead yet.

The Third Psychosis You Witnessed

A row of text like the *Star Wars* opening crawl scrolled on a big screen right behind my eyes, on repeat, in yellow, in white, in gold, bold.

The words crawled for a long time, etching themselves onto the dark wall of my inner skull, a sword-point dragging across porcelain.

The instructions were clear:

Remove sleeve. Pierce several times.

And it scrolled on and on and on and on and on and on and so I did, I removed my sleeve and pierced several times with a paring knife. *STAB! STAB STAB STAB!* The blade bypassed bone, and the knife point satisfyingly emerged from the underside of my skinny arm: straight through, clean. *Stab stab stab.* How many times is "several" anyway? The instructions didn't mention anything about stirring halfway through, so I sat completely still and let myself marinate in a doll-sized bloodbath, in my sparkly party dress, with sawdust in my hair, and the spider on the wall for company, and I watched the *Star Wars* crawl grad-   ually

                fade   in-

to   no-

      thing-

                            ness.

You found me eventually.

What the hell are you doing in the attic?

    I can't remem-

JESUS CHRIST, WHAT HAVE YOU DONE?!

    Well, it said "remove sleeve and pierce several times" so
    I did.

WHAT? NOT ON YOUR ARM, YOU SILLY COW!

    I was just following the instructions.

YOU ARE NOT A MICROWAVE MEAL!

    Sorry, but the instr-

YOU ARE NOT A FUCKING LASAGNE!

Every now and then you email me to remind me that I am not a lasagne.

"I am not a lasagne. I am not a microwave meal. I am not a lasagne. I am not a lasagne. I am not his problem anymore. I am not a lasagne." Tonight, this is the inner monologue that scrolls on a big screen right behind my catatonic eyes, on repeat, in yellow, in white, in gold, bold. "I am not a fucking lasagne."

Worried to Death (2)

It's absurd how I can no longer clink
a glass in cheers without thinking

of you. The image arrives automatically:
you, tangled in sweaty bedsheets, knife slicing

the top off a strawberry, plonking it into my drink
with ceremony, your face grinning gold, beaming

& me the next morning, discovering the knife secreted
in a pile of laundry where you'd hidden it from me.

Better to be safe than sorry.
I was always so sorry.

Strongbow Dark Fruits

*"Vous êtes belles mais vous êtes vides, leur dit-il
encore. On ne peut pas mourir pour vous."*
— Antoine de Saint-Exupéry

Out on the wonky patio
you read *Le Petit Prince* aloud
while I shaved your head, only pausing
to swig from my tin of tepid magenta cider,
to study the faded drawings, to brush clumps
of soft hair off the atlas of your suntanned back.

But I panicked once I knew
you were dangerously close
to *that* part, for I could not bear
to hear your voice telling me
that I was beautiful but empty,
that one could not die for me,
because it was true
& because I would have died for you
& that truth hurt *mon petit coeur.*

To get you to shut up,
I nicked the top of your left ear
with the razor blade.

It bled for days.

Anniversary Dinner

Like all of the worst party tricks,
it sounded more impressive than it was
in practice. The "lobster" aspect was just a tin
of bisque poured into a pre-diced tomato & shallot mix.
The crab was simply tipped out of a packet, the white meat
tossed for a hot minute in silky olive oil & fresh red chillies
that I'd ripped to bits between the tips of my trembling fingers.

But it looked fancy: coiled linguine presented on the only dish
in the house I hadn't chosen to break in a fit of rage or pain;
buttery garlic ciabatta sticks along the lip of the plate;
a [stolen] bottle of champagne in a [stolen] ice bucket;
our typically chaotic dining table cleared of scraps
of poetry & crosswords & final demand notices.

For years you had seen me cook up breakdowns in batches,
watched me store trauma in tupperware, prepped & ready
to be defrosted & reheated the moment my brain decided
our life had become too quiet. Still, you stood by
with a fire extinguisher as I experimented with baking
cupcakes made of reflexology & EMDR & magic
mushroom microdoses. Yet every effort at curing
the cerebral meat of me tasted burnt & toxic,
just fucked me up further, left me malnourished.

The thing I needed so badly was to be hooked
to an IV of fridge-cool sanity, to be force-fed peace

through a tube to the stomach. Instead I drank daily
from a hot spring of suicidal thinking, life-ruining
impulsivity, self-harming ideologies, catastrophe.

You saw doctors throw diagnosis after diagnosis
after medication after medication at me as if I were
a tiled kitchen wall, as if my psychiatric history was
spaghetti, all of us wondering if a fix for my madnesses
would ever stick, instead of slipping to the counter, flaccid.

But last week, my new menu had officially been
drawn up & laminated: mirtazapine, the apéritif,
to be consumed every morning. BPD, al dente
with a sprinkling of psychosis, suggested pairing:
olanzapine. C-PTSD, glazed in heavy, full-fat
anxiety. Sweet benzodiazepines for pudding
& zopiclone in lieu of coffee; too much sleep
as a treat to ease the insomnia, sedatives
to smother my delusions & compulsions,
to kill the crippling despair in me.

Is it done yet? Yes. Dinner is ready
& I know it's not perfect, but
I hope you'll still love it.

Textbook, Classic BPD

I came home one day to find you on the settee
reading a book that was written about me.

It was penned by some American doctors,
self-professed experts who have never met me

& it sets out to explain why I am the way I am,
to justify me. It had an ugly cover.

By the look on your face, I could tell that it didn't help you
to see me spread across the pages like that: dismembered

into tidy chapters, chunks of my spirit dissected into symptoms,
my behaviours boiled down to alarming statistics, my traumas

presented as tragic excuses, my soul turned into science
by careless strangers with superiority complexes.

Still, you'd made notes. Lots & lots of notes.
I plucked them out of your hand & off the floor & read them:

> *"Individuals with BPD are the psychological equivalent of people*
> *with third degree burns over 90% of their bodies. Lacking emotional*
> *skin, they feel agony at the slightest touch."*
> *so <u>everything hurts her</u> she is in pain <u>all the time</u> !!!*

*Splitting = when she thinks in extremes, black and white thinking, all
or nothing. She can't understand or see the grey middle ground.*

*Symptoms = emotional instability (yes) affective dysregulation (yes)
disturbed patterns of thinking (yes) cognitive distortions (yes)
perceptual distortions (yes esp when psychotic) impulsive behaviour
(always) intense but unstable relationships with others (YES)*

*73% with BPD attempt suicide at least once in their lifetimes.
She's already tried 4 times. Or 5? 14% complete the act.
The suicide success rate for people with BPD is higher than
any other psychiatric disorder. THIS IS WORRYING.*

I pulled the Zippo out of my back pocket & set all the notes on fire.
You were annoyed & impressed all at once, but mostly you were

in love. You told me that you were never going to leave me,
even if I told you to, even if I let you. I asked you

if the textbook told you to say that.
The smoke alarm was shrieking.

You picked a piece of burnt paper
out of my hair & shook your head.

The textbook was never seen again.

Wild Horses & Sugar Gliders

You mix my medication into a pot of vanilla yoghurt and instruct me on how to eat.

Open. Come on. That's it.
No, don't chew it, it's yoghurt, just get it down ya, fucksake.
There's a good girl.

Something is ringing, the trill rattles my bones—*brrrrr*—my skeleton vibrates but I can't locate the source of the noise. It hurts to move my eyeballs; my brain weighs the same as a grand piano. You find my phone and see who is calling me: it's the guy who you are (quite rightly) suspicious about. You pretend you didn't see who called but I see your aura change colour and you exhale too sharply.

I start shouting about needing a cigarette. You find my cigs and lighter and slowly walk me to the balcony, your hands on my elbows, steering me through the door frame. You light me up and hold me back, away from the edge. I keep dropping my cigarette. I cry. I ask you where the moon is, and you tell me that *it's up there somewhere but it's hiding*. I cry harder, furious that you can't summon the moon for me.

You scoop me up and carry me to bed. Somehow you manage to remove the ridiculous mini chandeliers that are threaded through my earlobes; you place them carefully on the bedside table on top of my dogeared *Agua Viva*. I am suddenly aware that I ought to brush my teeth, but I don't have the strength, and the idea leaves me as quickly as it arrived. I don't know what day it is, and I don't care. I don't know who I am. I don't know who you are. I don't know where I am. What is this? I just need everything to stop. What is this?! Who the fuck are you? What are you doing? I don't like it. I don't like this one bit. You magically produce a plastic syringe filled with oramorph syrup. I am so happy to see you. I tell you that I love you.

I   *love*   *you.*

You use your index finger to prise my bitten-to-ribbons lips apart, put the tip of the syringe into my mouth and slowly release the full plunger of liquid morphine. It is super-sweet, fake strawberry, it bites my teeth, *ouch. More,* I say. *One more.* You relent too easily, anything to please me. I slurp down the cloying morphine solution and imagine that I feel something close to happy. You arrange my deadweight body into the recovery position and tell me that I'm safe, that *everything's going to be fine*, that when I'm better *we'll go to the seaside*, that I *don't need to apologise*, that you're *here to look after* me. I ask you if we can adopt some sugar gliders instead of having kids. I don't know what your reply is, if you even replied at all, but I'm sure you would've said *yes, of course, Dolly,* because you love me too much. You smooth my hair and whisper-sing lyrics to songs by The Rolling Stones until I fall asleep.

My dreams are doused in the ever-present fear that the sicknesses that live in my brain, that create so much chaos and pain between us, will surely cause you to walk away one day — voluntarily, gladly, thankfully, you'll leave me. That, or I'll drag you down with me.

Either way, it's not looking pretty, and I am disappointed when I wake up with a pulse thirty-one hours later.

You're perched on the end of the bed and ask me if I want to look at the sugar gliders someone is selling on Gumtree. I have no idea what you're talking about. I don't even know what a sugar glider is.

Another Involuntary Section

Another ID wristband—tethered to Earth only by name & number.
Another plastic mattress—no sheets, no pillow, no other furniture.
Another locked room—unopenable from the inside, trapped in terror.

Pissed off policeman outside the door, playing games on his phone.
The words WHY, NO & HELP scratched onto the unbreakable
barred & wired window. The camera in the corner with the red light,

blinking incessantly, evil eye stalking me. A mix of old & fresh
blood on the walls. The smell of other people's piss, vomit, tears,
shame, the stench of my fear that permeates this hospital cell.

I am sitting on the sticky floor, digging bright red holes
in my palms—stigmata for the stigmatised. I do not know
how many hours or days or weeks I have been in here.

The door unlocks & I hide behind my sweat-drenched hair.
I am so fucking scared. *Hey Dolly.* But you… are here?
How are you feeling? I got you those noodles you like.

And a milkshake. And clean clothes. But… I was convinced
that you'd never want to see me again, not after this,
another appalling episode in which I "completely lost it."

You kiss my clammy cheek & hand me six lined pages, ripped
straight out of my notebook. They are blank. I am blank.
I thought you'd want to write, so I brought you a pen and paper.

I am blank. *But they wouldn't let me give you the pen.*
I am blank. *You know… in case…*
& both our hearts break in tandem.

"Breaking Up" in Soho

another strange night in purgatory
our faces torn between the heaven
of tipsy candlelight & the hell
of gaudy neon signs that curious
liminal state in which we existed
in love out of love somewhere
between agony & pain we were
really angry at each other for reasons
out of reach to me now I'd probably
done something stupid or had too many
feelings again that you couldn't take
but the safety of our cloistered sanctuary
in this cosy little restaurant we had
never been to before & the warmth
& comfort afforded by the melting
wax pillar that stood coyly between us
as we sat in quiet contentment falling
silently into respect for each other again
our bellies full of risotto & steak & rioja
neither of us daring to say
anything to disrupt this
rare piece of peace
to make the first move to utter
I think we should call it a day
look this has been fun but
the rhythmic blinking of electric
signs on the other side of the window

the liquid letters in brash colours
screaming 18+ touting London's finest
mags + dvds + toys + girls girls girls
& MASSAGE with a short-circuited M
the way the fluorescence fell on your face
(I could've screamed you looked like a saint)
dissipated my rage our rage it made us
wicked & in the mood for sabotage
but in a different way so we went to
a peep show instead & laughed our heads
right back & fucked on the night bus home
backseats top deck & you asked me to
marry you the next day & I said no
because I loved you so much
I told you that you deserved better
than me but now I'm not sure
if I really truly meant it
because in the end
you turned out
to be a prick.

~~That's Abuse~~ It Was An Accident

It was a sad thing to discover that
the sensation of your lit cigarette burying
its hot head in the pale crook of my arm
was the closest that I'd ever get
to ~~falling in love~~ touching the sun.

Haematoma

You counted my bruises—fifty-five—& I cried
because I detest the number five. You placed
your warm palm over the dandelion
disc that was blooming on my thigh
& laid your bitten lips upon
the swollen merlot shiner
radiating around my right eye.
For me, you made it fifty-three,
but I didn't deserve any.

Bio-Oil®

In the bathroom, you sighed
with your entire body weight
as you applied the viscous oil
in gentle circles onto the red & white
lines that brand my forearms & thighs.
I sucked the hot sting through the gaps
in my teeth, stared at the dead spider
in the dusty corner, wished I was her.

We're meant to do this morning & night
to encourage my mutilations to heal & fade,
but I let you touch me less & less these days.
You had to trick me into this with the promise
of wine & drugs afterwards. Wrapping my limbs
in cling film & tape, you said with odd optimism,

I want your scars to disappear
so that you can wear sleeveless tops
& shorts when it's hot outside,

but your hope was so misplaced. I replied,

I want to disappear
so that the sadness stops
& you can get on with your life.

What was that?

Ugh. Nothing, I lied & sighed & decided that
we are never doing this charade again. You & I
know this is a pointless exercise. I always find the knives.

Cereal for Dinner

Remember when the party was over?
When I was too much for you
& you were not enough for me.

During that time, when consciousness was simply too painful
for our sensitive souls, we consumed a carefully curated cocktail
of vodka, valium, propranolol & zopiclone, enough to induce
forced hibernation. We called it "silly self-care" because,
although it wasn't smart, it was necessary for survival.

Better to sleep through it, we decided, hoping
we'd wake invigorated, our old selves
again, unstoppable, mad
for & about each other.

We slept for days, weeks, through the coldest
months, seeing nobody, going nowhere, doing nothing
but sleeping, only occasionally waking to fuck & piss & smoke,
hazy in our fugue state, eyes glazed, hair stale with sweat & breath.
Then we'd take more pills, drink more booze, pass out cold again.
All that time spent refusing to live & refusing to die.
This self-inflicted coma was the closest I've ever felt
to ~~you~~ peace. I dreamt of nothing.

x

When we finally awoke from our ignorance
& went outdoors, hatched from our shells of rest,
we discovered that Spring had happened while we slept.
The only time that red & pink ever look good together is when
the cherry blossom trees have erupted outside the fire station.
I wonder what else we missed while we slept away those finite
& unwanted hours of ours. Later, when we were eating
cereal for dinner, we realised that nobody had missed us.
And, most terribly of all, we hadn't missed each other.

x

(I can still feel
the phantom ident
your body left
on the mattress.)

Casual Vandal

Remember when you painted that declaration

of love in huge letters across the old sea wall?

YOUR NAME <3 MY NAME

sprayed in blinding white along the weathered face

of the ancient granite flood defence. You led me there,

Arsenal scarf tied as a blindfold, then unveiled the graffiti

as if it had won the Turner Prize. You explained that it would

last longer than our lifetime, that everyone who approached

the island would see just how much I was adored by you.

You vandalised a protected landmark just so

every stranger would know that I belonged,

that my name was not one that stood

alone. Perhaps if I had been

impressed by this gesture

instead of utterly horrified,

we might have survived.

(Don't) Tell Me What To Do To Fix This

You'd always say to me,

>   *Don't be sad, baby,*

as if it was that easy.

x

>   You know I don't like being told what to do.
>
>   The stubborn child in me wakes up
>
>   when confronted with authority.
>
>   I'll do the opposite, just to spite you.

x

Maybe if you'd said to me,

>   *Don't be happy, baby,*

I would've tried desperately hard to be.

A Son First, Then A Daughter

I should've realised we weren't going to make it
when we were wandering around that big, empty house
out in the countryside one luminous afternoon in June.

We'd grown up by now: no more cocaine binges
& shoplifting sprees. Time to settle down,
get serious, get married, have babies.

Though you'd visibly aged (another thing I blamed
myself for), your own face was childlike that day, so full
of excitement & hope. You were babbling, saying things like,

Can you see yourself cooking dinner in this kitchen?
Your eyes, those searing blue blowtorch flames, were watching
our future children playing gleefully in the vast garden

(a son first, you'd insisted, then a daughter, as if I could arrange that
for you). You were envisioning a real future for us, one I couldn't
even permit myself to imagine, let alone see clearly in front of me.

x

I was *terrified* of a tiny version of us growing inside of me.
Scared of my soon-to-be-assumed role of "wife & mother"
with no time to write, no room to breathe, no space to be.
Internally screaming at the prospect of relentless mortgage payments.
Panicking that our babies might inherit my sadness/madness/nose.

Worrying about hypothetical meals being served on time
& accidentally murdering my orchids
& forgetting to pick the kids up from school
& never *quite* getting used to the absence of silence.

I was frightened that I'd feel stuck
in a life that wasn't truly mine
but I reasoned that it'd be fine
because I'd be stuck to you.

x

Later, when I explored the top floor of the house alone,
I quietly considered which room I would end my life in
if/when I chose to, assessing which fixtures were sturdy

enough to hang from & wondering what the freestanding
claw-foot bathtub would look like with red water spilling
over its gilt edges. "Well, at least the crimson flood of

my blood will complement the nursery,
which we are going to paint lemon yellow,"
I said aloud to nobody.

A Box of Frogs, A March Hare, A Cut Snake

Sometimes, I catch myself doing something "normal" like drinking a cup of tea & reading a newspaper, sitting nicely at the table with my feet on the ground & my back straight & my cheeks dry, concentrating on the paper in front of me but not thinking too deeply about its contents (flicking through the pages casually, pausing to frown about Syria or fume about Tories or tut at an unflattering photo of a D-list celebrity) & in that moment, in the act of doing something so mundane, I'm (and this is important) *not* thinking in a way that matches all of my madnesses—I'm not thinking with my BPD Brain or my Traumatised Brain or my Psychotic Brain or my Anxiety Brain, not thinking about bleeding out, not thinking about overdosing, not thinking about the beatings, not thinking about my father dying, not thinking about how

you're   definitely   100%   going   to   abandon   me.

No, in these moments of apparent normalcy, when I'm conducting myself like "a proper human being", doing nice little easy things, I'm *not* thinking about *any* of the everyday badness; I'm not thinking about the barrage of symptoms that come with these mental illnesses that wreak havoc on my body; I'm not thinking about the flashbacks & the what-ifs & the has-beens, the collection of untrained traumas that terrorise me daily—no. I'm busy doing "Normal People Things" with relative ease. So I will say to myself, *Aha! You were FINE for a minute there! Totally fine. Look at you, reading the newspaper like a sane person. Maybe you're not crazy? Maybe you're not crazy at all?!?!?!* & then

I   feel   like   a   fraud   because   I   am

either mad or not mad depending on a million different factors & a million different people who think in a million different ways. But, either way, I'm alive (but I wish I wasn't) & I'm going to die (but I wish I wasn't) & so I go back to what I was doing before I dared to attempt

to   Just   Be   Normal: I   go   back   to   lying

on the floor, in the dark, curled up, foetal, fists hitting my forehead (goawaygoawaygoaway), taunted once again by All of The Things that make me Bad/Sad/Mad. Later on I'll wake up & find that I'm being assaulted by the sun (how much time has passed?). I'll also discover that my hair is in my hands (I've ripped chunks out again) & I'll find that the newspaper has been taken off the table, unfolded & placed over me as a pathetic blanket (did I do this?) & the sound of my shallow breathing will make me vomit because that means I'm still alive & that is Not Good & I can't do It (I can't do This, I can't do It, I can't do any of It) so I'll just stay on the floor for four days until you get back from your trip & find my meds & put me to bed, & I'll think about all the people who told me that I'm fine & I'll think that

many   of   them   are   just   as   mad   as   me.

God, They Look Happy

Remember that time
Sunday afternoon
when you wound me up
over fuck-knows-what
probably some imaginary
slight that hurt me too deeply
so I upended my pint of overpriced
Bloody Mary over your hungover head?

At first you were fuming
your shirt was ruined
& you looked like a victim
in a crime scene on tv
covered in fake claret
& your face wore a thin coat
of red hurt & the spice
& citrus stung your eyes
but the stick of celery
that garnished the drink
had landed so pathetically
on the floor by your feet
we both looked at it
& just had to piss ourselves
laughing collapsing
at the ridiculousness of it & everyone
in the pub garden was watching us
& that woman said miserably

God, they look happy

& then I felt bad
so I grabbed
your Bloody Mary & poured it
over my own head & the celery sticks
crunched under our feet as we kissed
through the red liquid teeth knocking
still laughing into each other's mouths
hysterically our faces split in half
by fat drunk-in-love grins
wiping red tears from
each other's cheeks

& I said, *You've got tomato juice on your new trainers*
& you said, *Well, you've got tabasco on your tits.*

Yeah, I haven't ordered another Bloody Mary since.

Self Portrait of Sorrys

I can only apologise for turning up to your birthday party
wrecked & weeping, wrists bandaged haphazardly, looking like
a blood-bloated flea that had been cut in half with a fingernail
instead of looking spectacular, like a bakery window display
on its opening day or city snowfall in July. I'm sorry for being
the wrong kind of startling, the literal kind of arresting. I'm sorry
that the dregs of this knock-off Chanel No.5 does not mask the scent
of the everyday fury & disillusionment that spurts in bursts from
my Piccadilly-Line-grime-choked pores & I've already apologised
countless times for coming home smelling like another man's pillow.
I'm sorry that I won't be able to hold you when you're grieving
my death — that is so fucking typical of me, to not be there for you
when I'm dead & you need me. I am sorry that I feel like running
with undone laces & fresh blisters & I'm really sorry that my kisses
taste like broken diamonds; I know that isn't what you ordered, isn't
what you signed up for, was never what you expected & I'm sorry
that you lost the receipt, that you'll get no refund, no recompense
for the life you spent on me. I'm sorry that I sound like fishnet tights
snagging on barbed wire & that every flicker of my heartbeat serves
as a siren, threatening endless disasters impending. I apologise
for containing all of the lives that you are too afraid to live.
Believe me: I, too, wish I wasn't like this.
You do still love me though. Don't you?

Do You Still Have My Wisdom Tooth?

You wiped the cobwebs off
those rusty pliers from the shed
said *Open wide* & wrenched
it out of my mouth. The *crack*
shot lightning down the street
& birds fell out of trees.

I got it. Are you happy?

I spat & nodded, jaw sore as
you held my bloody wisdom
tooth in your trembling hand
chunk of decayed porcelain
menstruating pearl
& said,

Look. The source of your grief.

You were talking
about the tooth
but I heard it as if
you were talking
about yourself.
I let you keep it,

As a treat, to go with all the other pieces of me.

Jump

I know you remember how my laughter broadcast itself
as we drunkenly cartwheeled down the silent corridor
of another nameless hotel. You remember the sound of
my apple sourz cackle. You remember how my happiness
echoed all along those ugly hallways. You remember that
another guest begged us to *please SHUT the FUCK up* because
we were rioting, spraying each other with fire extinguishers,
shouting declarations of love to one another, soaked in foam.
You remember telling me to jump down that flight of stairs,
telling me to trust you, that you'd catch me. And I did,
and I did, and you did. You remember that you promised me
you'd make me happy. And you did. You remember that
you promised me you'd never let me go. But you did.

Listening to an 'end credits' playlist & feeling sick about the
kiss that never happened

Tonight the wide Parma Violet sky demands
to be written as poetry. Every time
the clouds decide to dress themselves
in matching crushed-lilac outfits
like this, my poor score-keeping body
returns to Highgate Station carpark,
when the cool January afternoon sat
behind a lavender filter & I whispered
something along the lines of *I need you*
to kiss me like you'll never see me again
(because when you're twenty, you believe
your life to be some tragic indie movie)
(because I had it set in my mind to die,
to take my life that night) & you replied,
What the fuck. No. That's so stupid & refused,
just hugged me weakly & drove away,
left me gutted on the platform, convinced
the world had ended. Did you know then,
under that powdery purple firmament,
that our last kiss had already happened?
That that swift press of our tired lips
over milky tea that morning had been *it*?
Because I certainly didn't.
Though perhaps I should've —
we got caught in too many sticky webs
spun of other people's judgement,
got caught in faking sanity & safety only

to be confronted with their opposites.
Our love became just another
crumpled betting slip, nothing won
but broken promises & bitterness;
we had lost the bet we made on ourselves
all those years before. The sky knew
it was over before I'd even admitted it —
the beginnings of a bruise already
aching beyond the train window,
a great mauve promise of apocalypse.

Brewer Street

Last week I found myself walking past our old flat on Brewer Street
& remembered all those dawns we spent putting the world to wrongs,
sitting side by side on the filthy kitchen floor, the lino peeling,
tap dripping in time with my exhausted heartbeat, drinking
Johnnie Walker Black Label out of cracked teacups, arguing
about who is the best Beatle, discussing
the pros & cons of freedom.

The cons of being free have long stayed with me,
even though you didn't. I believe this loneliness
will be the death of me; not suicide, not grief,
but solitude, having no choice but to exist
in this brain on my own. Still, I think,
honestly, we'd both say now,
Thank god we fell apart.

Wouldn't we?

Fuck Forever

Forever's never guaranteed
but still you wrote the F-word
inside every card you ever gave to me.

I'll love you forever x x x

I cannot bring myself to throw these cards away.
I stow them in a shoebox in my wardrobe,
to be read on rainy days when I miss you
so much my ribcage aches. They are proof
that Forever once existed, that immortality
was possible for us. Or for me, anyway.

Me and you, forever and a day x x x

One day, when I'm stronger or stranger or older or braver,
I'll shred these fanciful notions of infinity. These sentiments
were once a thing of utter beauty to me; words I've memorised
to the same extent as I did the freckles on your shoulders & the list
of your favourite biscuits (from god tier to shit); romanticisms
authored by the great love of my disastrous life; lines that once
kept me alive but that have since been murdered,
all the fantasies of Forever rendered falsehoods
in the wake of our ending.

Forever yours x x x

Yes, I *will* bin your sweet words eventually. I'll probably build
a bonfire & throw the remnants of our love on it, fan the flames
with my hurricane of shame, pour on your chloroform kisses,
inhale the death-scent of us. One day, someday, but not today.

BPD revels in telling me I'm *unlovable*,
that no one would ever want me.
Today, I need to remember that
somebody loved me once.
That once, I was loved.
I was *loved*.

And what a thing it was
to have been loved
by you.

Acknowledgements

Thank you to the editors of the following journals for publishing early versions of these poems:

Worried to Death (1) / Worried to Death (2) – One Hand Clapping
Gagged & Bound / A Son First, Then A Daughter – Sledgehammer Lit
Wild Horses & Sugar Gliders – Damnation Lit
Another Involuntary Section – Mental Inkness
"Breaking Up" in Soho – Anthropocene
~~That's Abuse~~ It Was An Accident – Emerge Literary Journal
Cereal for Dinner – Mausoleum Press
(Don't) Tell Me What To Do To Fix This – Dust Poetry
Jump – streetcake magazine
Fuck Forever – Green Ink Poetry

About the Author

HLR (she/her) is a prize-winning working-class poet from North London. Her debut collection *History of Present Complaint* (First Cut Poetry) was longlisted in the Poetry Book Awards 2022. She is a commended winner of the National Poetry Competition 2021, won the Desmond O'Grady International Poetry Competition 2021, and was longlisted in the Plough Prize 2022 and Mslexia Poetry Competition 2022. Her work has been published by *The London Magazine, Poetry Wales, Bad Lilies,* and many others.

Read more of her work at www.treacleheart.com and find her on Twitter: @HLRwriter.

Milton Keynes UK
Ingram Content Group UK Ltd.
UKHW040843230923
429253UK00004B/79